Bedrock Bookkeeper
Business Success System

From Myths to Money

How to Turn Old Ideas about
Business Failure into Massive Success

Joe DiChiara,
CPA/Entrepreneur

www.BedrockBookkeepersBusinessSuccessSystem.com

Published by
RockStar Publishing House
32129 Lindero Canyon Road, Suite 205
Westlake Village, CA 91361
www.rockstarpublishinghouse.com

Manufactured in the United States of America,
or in the United Kingdom when distributed elsewhere.

DiChiara, Joe
From Myths to Money: How to turn old ideas
about business failure into massive success

Paperback: 9781938015267
eBook: 9781938015274

Cover design by: Joe Potter
Cover photo by: Yoti Telio
Interior design: Scribe Inc.
Photo credits: Yoti Telio

www.bedrockbookkeeping.com

The objective of this book is to identify, explain, and provide answers to the myths about the epidemic of small business failures around the world while providing pragmatic solutions to these issues. I will dispel the common myths the public has been programmed to believe about what it takes to start, run, and grow a successful small business.

—Joe DiChiara, CPA/Entrepreneur

Contents

Foreword

According to Bloomberg, 8 out of 10 entrepreneurs who start businesses fail within the first 18 months. A catastrophic 80% crash and burn!

Joe DiChiara in his book *From Myths to Money* can help you become one of the 20% who actually achieve success.

Joe helps the reader understand that the myths we grew up believing are actually most of the reasons those small business fail!

He points out why believing these *conventional wisdom* beliefs limit your success and why they are ALL MYTHS!

Business moves fast and so does this book. In only 96 pages Joe provides all the knowledge you need to achieve lasting success in your business.

For example:

> *"In an attempt to remain in control and save money, owners take on tasks they are not good at or do not enjoy. As a result they have less time to spend on what they are good at doing."*

"Developing a 'Definite Chief Aim'—A simple three-part statement is provided that defines where, how and what you are setting out to do."

"Clear Directions on how you can succeed in a bad economy."

"Learn how to create Mastermind Alliances and turn competitors into partners."

Joe Dichiara's book *From Myths to Money* will absolutely give you the keys you need to be in that elite and successful TOP 20%.

Karen Strauss
President, Strauss Consultants
Author of *Publishing for Entrepreneurs: Secrets from a New York Publisher*
New York, NY

Acknowledgments

We can never achieve true success on our own. There have been scores of people in my life who have served as powerful examples for me and/or coached me along the way. I will be forever grateful to all of them.

Besides the obvious, my family, I want to thank Vinny D., a man I am certain was sent by God. This extraordinary man counseled me in business and my professional life over the past thirty-five-plus years. If it was not for Vince, I may have never become a CPA and gained the invaluable experience I have today. He also taught me by example the importance of giving back, not only monetarily but with his time.

I want to thank my brother from another mother, Craig Duswalt. It's no coincidence that Vinny D. advised me early on of the benefits of joining a college fraternity. I joined the Sigma Gamma fraternity up in S.U.N.Y. Oswego, which Craig was a member of. That turned out to be one of the best experiences of my life. Craig "appeared" back in my life a few years ago and introduced me to his RockStar System for Success and his tremendous entourage of RockStars.

Acknowledgments

These RockStars have helped me connect the dots and fill in the missing pieces. That has made all the difference.

Thanks to Wallace Wattles for writing *The Science of Getting Rich,* which introduced me to the concept of "Thinking a Certain Way." Thank you, Andrew Carnegie, for challenging Napoleon Hill to prove his theory of success. And, finally, I want to thank Mr. Hill for taking Mr. Carnegie up on his challenge. Mr. Hill's *The Law of Success* connected perfectly to Mr. Wattles's *The Science of Getting Rich.* For me, the instructions outlined in these literary works have led me to develop a kinder, gentler business and personal life with virtually endless opportunities.

This book is my first step in paying forward what I have learned from those brilliant minds.

Introduction

For over thirty years, false beliefs helped drive my business and personal life. That all started to change in July 2007 when I read *The Science of Getting Rich* by Wallace Wattles. According to Mr. Wattles, most of what I was taught about becoming successful in business were misguided half-truths. A lack of capital; a bad economy; it's not what you know but who you know; and so on were not the true reasons for small business failures. The book made me think about my previous thirty years of business experience. Everything I had learned in school, in life, and my experience in working with thousands of small businesses was turned upside down.

It made me wonder why the majority of small businesses fail when they really didn't have to. What about the businesses that don't "fail" but just barely get by? What happened to the American Dream and the Pursuit of Happiness? Someone told me a long time ago that people can achieve anything they put their minds to, and I believed it. I believe that now more than ever, but it took almost thirty years to find out how. I learned why so many good, hardworking people with good ideas and good intentions were destined to fail or just barely survive.

Why do some people have the ability to overcome all the apparent obstacles other people claim are the reasons for their lack of success?

In his book, Mr. Wattles says that people with little education and little money can get rich. Even people with absolutely no talent, no connections, and no resources can become unbelievably successful. On the other side of the coin, people who start with plenty of money, talent, beauty, connections, and education can wind up complete failures. Some people also become successful in bad economic times while others fail in good economic times. How do you explain this?

Before we get into the details, success and failure need to be defined. Most people correlate money with success and a lack of it with failure, and to a certain extent, that is true. I believe that while money can be a measure of success, having no money does not equate to failure. There are also different levels of success and successful achievements that do not necessarily define or lead to success. A person can also be a big success in one area of their life and a complete failure in other areas.

Understanding this and the fact that this book is entirely my view, let's assume that in these pages, success and failure are completely defined as I see it. You can agree or disagree; it doesn't matter. In other words, my definition cannot be wrong, just as yours cannot be wrong. Each person has a subjective definition of success and failure. Success for you may not be success for me.

There are also *objective* definitions.

Merriam-Webster (www.merriam-webster.com)

Definition of Success

1. Degree or measure of succeeding
2. Favorable or desired outcome; also: the attainment of wealth, favor, or eminence

Examples of Success

1. Success came easily to him.
2. She is country music's most recent *success.*
3. The growth of the tourism industry is one of the city's great *successes.*

Definition of Failure

1. Omission of occurrence or performance; *specifically:* a failure to perform a duty or expected action <*failure* to pay the rent on time>
2. A state of inability to perform a normal function <kidney *failure*>—compare heart failure (2): an abrupt cessation of normal functioning <a power *failure*>
3. A fracturing or giving way under stress <structural *failure*>

4. Lack of success
5. A failing in business: bankruptcy
6. A falling short: deficiency <a crop *failure*>

Examples of Failure

1. He became discouraged by his repeated *failure* in business.
2. He was often crippled by his fear of *failure.*
3. The accident was caused by engine *failure.*
4. The patient was suffering from heart *failure.*
5. The accident was caused by a *failure to use* proper procedures.
6. She was criticized for *failure to follow* directions.
7. The drought caused crop *failures.*
8. He felt like a *failure* when he wasn't accepted into law school.
9. The scheme was a complete *failure.*

Dictionary.com

Definition of Success

1. The favorable or prosperous termination of attempts or endeavors.
2. The attainment of wealth, position, honors, or the like.
3. A successful performance or achievement: The play was an instant success.
4. A person or thing that is successful: She was a great success on the talk show.

Definition of Failure

1. An act or instance of failing or proving unsuccessful; lack of success: His effort ended in failure. The campaign was a failure.
2. Nonperformance of something due, required, or expected: a failure to do what one has promised; a failure to appear.
3. A subnormal quantity or quality; an insufficiency: the failure of crops.
4. Deterioration or decay, especially of vigor, strength, and so on. The failure of her health made retirement necessary.
5. A condition of being bankrupt by reason of insolvency.

My Definitions

My definitions of success and failure are as follows:

Success: Success is the attainment of true happiness, peace, serenity, and freedom from financial insecurity. It is the ability to do what you want, when you want, whenever you want.
Failure: Giving up.

Take some time and review the definitions again and ask yourself whether you consider yourself "successful." If you're anything like me, you will have more questions. It's not really a yes or no answer. For me, it was yes in some areas and no in others. When I started looking at my career, there were many successes but I felt that I'd never fulfilled my true potential. The reason for that was made apparent to me while taking a Napoleon Hill course, *The Law of Success,* during June 2010. It happened exactly the way Napoleon Hill said it would in *Think and Grow Rich,* an audiobook I'd listened to over twenty-five years ago. I never forgot those words: "It would hit me like bolt of lightning." It was so obvious to me and so simple when I finally realized exactly what he was talking about.

So once I understood how it worked, I knew that the only question was, how high did I want to raise the bar in my own success? That's really the only question for you as well. How high do you want to raise the bar in your business and your life?

Once you define what you want to do and *know* it can be done, what will you choose to be successful at? Aim high! If you know it can be done, why not? Aim high, very high!

Famous Quotes about Success

Frederick B. Wilcox: Progress always involves risk. You can't steal second base and keep your foot on first.

J. C. Penney: Unless you are willing to drench yourself in your work beyond the capacity of the average man, you are just not cut out for positions at the top.

Mahatma Gandhi: As human beings, our greatness lies not so much in being able to remake the world . . . as in being able to remake ourselves.

Richard Bach: The more I want to get something done, the less I call it work.

Confucius: The superior man is modest in his speech but exceeds in his actions.

CHAPTER 1

The Plight of the Small Business Owner

It is a fact that only about one in twenty individuals achieves any level of real success. My education and business experience have showed me that there are two main explanations for this:

1. Most people don't know they can be successful.
2. Most people who believe they can be successful don't know exactly how to do it.

I believe that the one in twenty figure is abysmal and there is no *real* reason it can't be fifteen or sixteen out of twenty. If you fit into category one or two, I hope that this book will provide an idea of what you can do to get on the road to success.

I found that one of my purposes in life is to eliminate these two small obstacles by:

1. Proving that anyone can be successful if they want to be.
2. Showing them exactly how they can be successful.

People start businesses for a variety of reasons:

- Freedom
- Entrepreneurial spirit
- The opportunity for success
- Passion
- Necessity

Very few people have the benefit of really knowing what it's like to actually run a business. They often run into what I call "the plight of the small business owner."

Most people who start a business possess a skill or talent for creating a product or providing a service that has value. A carpenter builds stuff, a chef cooks food, and an auto mechanic repairs and maintains cars. They are good at what they do, and they can find people who are willing to pay them. Unfortunately, they often mistake this for being able to start and run a business.

What happens approximately 95 percent of the time is this:

1. Owners generate revenue.
2. Word of mouth, advertising, and marketing efforts produce more customers/clients and thus more activity.

3. In an attempt to remain "in control" and to save money, owners take on tasks that they
   - are not experienced in
   - are not good at
   - do not enjoy

   Some of these tasks include but are not limited to bookkeeping, payroll, marketing, general administration, web design, graphics, social media, etc.
4. They run out of time.

This is the point at which many businesses fail. Often, owners try to compensate by:

1. Working more hours
2. Asking family members and friends with limited experience to handle the time-consuming tasks listed in number 3 above

There are two main reasons businesses remain in this holding pattern:

1. Owners don't know there is a solution.
2. They don't know how to implement the solution.

The paradox is that by being good at what they do, entrepreneurs inevitably acquire more business and create more activity. The paradox is that the activity leads to the entrepreneur running out of time and being spread too thin. This invariably leads to inefficiencies in the business but, more important, takes owners away from what they excel in—the craft that allowed them to start the business to begin with. They no longer spend enough time building stuff, cooking food, or repairing and maintaining cars.

When the builder/carpenter is doing his own payroll, he is wasting precious time that should be spent building. When the chef is building his Facebook fan page, he is not cooking, and when the mechanic is building a website, he is not working on cars. At this point, these business owners have reached a ceiling in their business.

Unfortunately, the majority of these businesses fail. Growth requires capital, and because these businesses have been built without any real foundation, they are destined to collapse like a house of cards. These businesses are rife with inefficiencies that can never be fully overcome. Cash flow is no longer sufficient to pay bills. Owners have to make a hard choice: Do they pay employees and vendors or do they pay their taxes and themselves? They begin to cut corners, which is reflected in their output and their general state of mind. The negative energy rips through these businesses like waves engulfing everyone—employees, vendors, customers, and inevitably, their family and friends.

Business owners are then faced with another hard choice: downsize to survive or raise the capital to stay in business (see "The Paradox of Money" in chapter 2). Most of the time, even if they can obtain it, the capital is wasted. The owners are stuck with closing down or just barely making enough to survive on top of paying the new debt. They are technically bankrupt. A very small percentage of these businesses are able to overcome these obstacles and achieve success. Sadly, because of their determination, most of these entrepreneurs struggle their entire lives, never realizing the real American Dream. For them, "the Pursuit of Happiness" was a myth.

Chapter 2

Myth #1

Lack of Capital

Most of my life I believed, as do many people, that a basic lack of capital was the number-one reason most businesses fail. My belief was based on what I was taught in school, my experience as a CPA, and information published in a multitude of business publications. The truth is that some of the most successful people in history started out broke or with very little capital. Henry Ford, J. K. Rowling, Harland Sanders (KFC), and countless others started with nothing but an idea. How do you explain that? Luck? I don't think so. History has proven over and over that a lack of capital does not equal business failure. I believe that many times having capital can actually be a detriment to business success. Having a tight budget can teach the business owner how important it is to keep expenses low and to come up with creative ways to handle situations that pop up.

The Paradox of Money

I recently sat down with a client who stated that when he first started his business, he got hit with $10,000 of unexpected expenses. He said, "If I'd only had $20,000 to start with, I would be OK today." Instead, he has spent the last year "just trying to get out of the original hole."

I told him, "If you had the twenty thousand to start with, you'd be another twenty thousand in the hole because you would have spent all that money and still would have wound up right where you are now." I know this because I have seen it happen all too often. Sometimes the worst thing an entrepreneur can have is money. Far too often it gets wasted.

Experience has taught me that focusing on money is like chasing cats. The more you chase them, the more they scatter. If you focus on what the cats want, like milk and food, they will find you. When you stop chasing the cat, it magically appears. It wasn't until I stopped focusing on making enough money and instead focused on my job that I was able to turn my business and my life around. When I stopped thinking "I need money," things started to change. I did not do that consciously at first. It was more of an evolution of thought. When I was able to put the final piece of the puzzle together, it all started making sense. My bills were being paid as a result of my new way of thinking. My whole career was spent thinking that if I could only make a little more money, I would be successful. The paradox was that no matter how much I made, I always had the same mentality: if I could only make a little more.

Solutions to the Lack of Capital

Take Money Out of the Equation.

Forget about money! I don't mean to literally forget about it; just take it out of the success equation. Look, it's a fact that you want and need money. Unless you're the next Mother Teresa—and even she needed money for her cause—you need lots and lots of money. If you live where I live, you probably need more money than most. If you have any kids, you need even more. You need money to buy things, own things, get out of debt, go places, and help your family and friends, among other things. This all takes money—a lot of it. So why state the obvious? One of the first steps I ask new clients to take is to list all their personal and business goals. At the top of most peoples' list is to make X amount or gross Y amount of money. Let's just assume that we all want and need plenty of money. The truth is that even the Internal Revenue Service states that if you are not in business for a profit, you are not a business. They will classify your "business" as a hobby. That's a fact. Look it up.

The real point here is that when you are preoccupied with your lack of money, chances are good that you will continue to live with a lack of money. I believe that if you do acquire capital without a firm business foundation, chances are that you will not put it to good use. The solution is to *take $$$ out of the equation.* Stop believing that a lack of cash is keeping you down and start focusing on your passion, your product or service, and your customers—the really important aspects of your business—and the money will follow. It *must* follow.

Barter for Services.

There are plenty of people in the same situation who could use your products and/or services, and if each of you had the cash, you might do business together. *Take $$$ out of the equation.* Do business, put a dollar value on the exchange, and keep a running balance of its value. You can do direct barter with people you know or join a barter "club." There are plenty of national and regional barter companies that offer different methods of trading. Most of them do charge cash fees for the service, so shop around for one that suits your needs.

Use Guerilla Marketing.

There is a lot of information on methods and ideas about guerilla marketing. The book by Jay Conrad Levinson *Guerilla Marketing* is worth much more than its weight in gold. The idea is to get the word out while spending little or no money. Some suggestions are spreading your message via word of mouth; putting a flyer in with your bills; posting your business cards on bulletin boards at car washes, libraries, cafés, etc. Use your imagination. You don't *always* have to spend money to get your message out there.

Get Creative.

Tap into the awesome power of your own mind. One of our most magnificent gifts is our power to create something from nothing. Everything that was ever created started with an idea. Every single thing you see has the same origin: *thought.* You may need capital at some point, but Henry Ford did not let that stop him from blanketing America with horseless carriages. Think about it. As Napoleon Hill said, *Think and Grow Rich!*

Be Determined.

Successful people never let a small detail such as the lack of capital get in their way. There are countless examples of individuals who were once totally broke and then became wildly successful. One of the underlying qualities in *all* of these people was their ability to stick with it no matter what. See the special bonus chapter by Larry Broughten, "Be Tenacious!," at the end of this book.

CHAPTER 3

Myth #2

Lack of Resources

If I only had _____ I could have _____ and then I would have _____. Fill in the blanks. Excuses, excuses, excuses. Woe is me. Successful entrepreneurs go and get it; they don't complain about not having it. They find a way, and if they can't find it, they create it.

How Did They Do It?

Andrew Carnegie came to the United States with no money, no education, no connections, and no "resources." How did he become one of the richest, most powerful men in history? Harland Sanders of KFC fame was bankrupt and on Social Security. All he had was a secret recipe. Martin Luther King Jr. had a dream. The Wright brothers owned a bicycle shop, while Professor Langley had the vast resources of the United States and academia at his disposal for his quest to create a "flying machine." None of these men had any resources, with the exception of Professor Langley, yet they became extremely successful. Professor Langley had every resource available at his disposal, yet he was unsuccessful. How do you explain this?

Solutions to the Lack of Resources

Develop a "Definite Chief Aim."

The starting point for all success is what Andrew Carnegie called a Definite Chief Aim—a simple, three-part statement that defines where, how, and what you are setting out to do. This is *the* most important step you must take in any endeavor and is much more of a process than a goal or mission statement. I believe that a Definite Chief Aim, combined with autosuggestion, is what Napoleon Hill was referring to when he came up with the title of his book *Think and Grow Rich*. This was the "lightning bolt" that hit me in July 2010, which set me on course for my present journey. For more on a Definite Chief Aim, see the special offer toward at the end of this book.

Develop a Burning Desire to Succeed.

Andrew Carnegie believed that our dominant thoughts are what drive us. Since we can choose what we think, we can in effect create a driving force, a burning desire. You can actually train your mind to take a desire and transform it into a burning desire through autosuggestion. The powerful tool of autosuggestion can take an idea and a goal and turn it into an obsession. This was the key to Napoleon Hill's firm belief in *Think and Grow Rich*. Think about something long enough and hard enough, and you can train your mind to work toward that goal, even when you are consciously doing something else. In other words, your subconscious is working toward that goal 24/7.

Definition of Autosuggestion from Dictionary.com

au·to·sug·ges·tion
noun, Psychology

Suggestion arising from oneself, as the repetition of verbal messages as a means of changing behavior.

Definition of Autosuggestion from Merriam-Webster (www.merriam-webster.com)

au·to·sug·ges·tion
noun

An influencing of one's own attitudes, behavior, or physical condition by mental processes other than conscious thought: self-hypnosis.

Origins

From www.wikipedia.org

Autosuggestion is a psychological technique that was developed by apothecary Émile Coué in the late nineteenth century and early twentieth century.

Coué graduated with a degree in pharmacology in 1876 and worked as an apothecary at Troyes from 1882 to 1910. When he began working at Troyes, he quickly discovered what later came to be known as the placebo effect. He became known for reassuring his clients by praising each remedy's efficiency and leaving a small positive notice with each given medication. Coué noticed that in certain cases he could improve the efficiency of a given medicine by praising its effectiveness to the patient. He realized that those patients to whom he praised the medicine had a noticeable improvement when compared to patients to whom he said nothing. This began Coué's exploration of the use of hypnosis and the power of the imagination. In 1901, he began to study under Ambroise-Auguste Liébeault and Hippolyte Bernheim, two leading exponents of hypnosis. After completing his tutelage, he began relying on hypnosis to treat patients.

From www.britannica.com

Émile Coué (born Feb. 26, 1857, Troyes, Fr.–died July 2, 1926, Nancy), French pharmacist who in 1920 at his clinic at Nancy introduced a method of psychotherapy character-ized by frequent repetition of the formula, "Every day, and in every way, I am becoming better and better." This method of autosuggestion came to be called Couéism.

An apothecary at Troyes from 1882 to 1910, Coué in 1901 began to study under Ambroise-Auguste Liébeault and Hippolyte Bernheim, leading exponents of hypnosis. Although stressing that he was not primarily a healer but one who taught others to heal themselves, Coué claimed to have effected organic changes through autosuggestion.

The Birth of Autosuggestion

Coué still believed in the effects of medication, but he also believed that our mental state was able to affect and even amplify the action of these medications. He ob-served that his patients who used his mantra-like con-scious suggestion, "Every day, in every way, I'm getting better and better" (French: *Tous les jours à tous points de vue je vais de mieux en mieux*), replacing their "thoughts of illness" with a new "thoughts of cure" could augment their medication plan. According to Coué, repeating words or images enough times causes the "subconscious" to absorb them. In contrast to Coué's opinion, Shultz believed autogenic training was a method for influenc-ing one's autonomic nervous system, not the so-called subconscious.

The Coué Method

The Coué method centers on a routine repetition of this particular expression according to a specified ritual, in a given physical state, and in the absence of any sort of allied mental imagery, at the beginning and at the end of each day. Unlike a commonly held belief that a strong conscious constitutes the best path to success, Coué maintained that curing some of our troubles requires a change in our subconscious/unconscious thought, which can only be achieved by using our imagination. Although stressing that he was not primarily a healer but one who taught others to heal themselves, Coué claimed to have effected organic changes through autosuggestion.

Underlying Principles

Coué thus developed a method that relied on the belief that *any idea exclusively occupying the mind turns into reality,* although only to the extent that the idea is within the realm of possibility. For instance, a person without hands will not be able to make them grow back. However, if a person firmly believes that his or her asthma is disappearing, then this may actually happen, as far as the body is actually able to physically overcome or control the illness. On the other hand, thinking negatively about the illness (e.g., "I am not feeling well") will encourage both mind and body to accept this thought.

Developing positive affirmations about what you want to achieve and employing the science of autosuggestion will produce a burning desire to achieve your goal that is so strong you will actually derive energy from it. You will wake in the morning without an alarm clock because your mind will be so trained that it cannot wait to start fulfilling your desire. This burning desire will be so strong that you'll lose all track of time because you do not have time to be tired or look at a clock. It seems as if it is all you think about. Nothing in the world matters as much as this burning desire.

What I just described might sound similar to how you feel and act when you first fall in love. In a sense, you can train your mind to be in tune with your heart so that your objective becomes almost obsessional. That is why auto-suggestion is such a powerful tool.

CHAPTER 4

Myth #3

A Lack of Connections

Did you ever hear the term "six degrees of separation"? The idea is that if you list all the people you know, and all the people they know, and all the people *they* know, by the sixth level, everyone in the world is connected. OK, so if I want to connect to Warren Buffett, all I really have to do is spend enough time and effort going up the food chain and eventually I can meet the man who I think will help me become unbelievably successful. Really? I'm not sure if the theory is correct, and even if it is, so what? Maybe knowing Warren Buffett *could* help me, but maybe knowing him would only do me as much good as reading what he has to say.

It's Not Always about Who You Know.

Not many people are born into rock stardom or a royal family. In the movie *Wall Street,* Bud Fox (Charlie Sheen) is obsessed with getting to the top and sets his sights on connecting with corporate raider Gordon Gekko (Michael Douglas). Bud is successful in connecting with Gordon, but at the expense of the values he learned from his father. The price is more than he bargained for, and eventually he decides it isn't worth it after all. I realize that *Wall Street* was just a movie, but it does paint a very good picture of what people are willing to do to get to the top and become "successful."

At age twelve, Steve Jobs decided to call one of the legends of Palo Alto—Bill Hewlett, one of the founders of Hewlett Packard—to find some electronic parts.

From the Hewlett Packard Website (www.hp.com/retiree/history/founders/hewlett/ quotes.html#generosity)

On Bill's Generosity

When he was in eighth grade, Steve Jobs decided to build a frequency counter for a school project and needed parts. Someone suggested that he call Bill Hewlett. Finding a William Hewlett in the telephone book, the 12-year-old Jobs called and asked, "Is this the Bill Hewlett of Hewlett-Packard?" "Yes," said Bill. Jobs made his request. Bill spent some time talking to him about his project. Several days later, Jobs went to HP and picked up a bag full of parts that Bill had put together for him. Subsequently, Jobs landed a summer job at HP. He later went on to cofound Apple Computer.

I guess that at twelve, Jobs didn't realize he was calling someone whom most people would consider off limits. I find the fact that he found him in the phone book pretty comical. Who would have the guts to call one of the most renowned inventors and businessmen of the time just to find some electronic parts? I propose that this is just one of the characteristics that made Steve Jobs who he was. At twelve, to Steve Jobs, Bill Hewlett was just a guy who could get him some parts.

That phone call eventually led Jobs to get a summer job at HP where he met Steve Wozniak; the two went on to form Apple Computer (now Apple Inc.). The interesting thing is that although Jobs and Wozniak created the Apple computer while working at HP, Hewlett Packard had no involvement in Apple. In fact, as an employee of HP, Wozniak was required to offer his invention to his employer who had the right of first refusal. HP had no interest in the Apple, which left Jobs and Wozniak free to create what eventually became the world's most valuable company.

Andrew Carnegie opened the doors of the most successful people in the world at the time for Napoleon Hill, yet that did not help Mr. Hill become successful. In fact, after twenty years of studying success and knowing people such as Henry Ford, Thomas Edison, and President Woodrow Wilson, he found himself full of knowledge but no real success. In fact, he was broke! It wasn't until he started applying the success principles he developed to his own life that he actually became successful. As Hill himself stated, knowledge by itself is worth nothing. Applied knowledge is what gets results. So much for having the right connections.

Solutions to a Lack of the Right Connection

Prove Yourself Worthy.

Get out there and prove to the people around you that you are serious about your business. Keep putting your positive message out there. Be persistent and passionate about what you are doing. If you truly believe in yourself, the connections will actually come to you.

Allow the Law of Attraction to Work.

Like attracts like. We are magnets attracting the kind of people we have set our minds on becoming.

Surround Yourself with Successful People.

Water seeks its own level. My grandmother used to say, "You can judge someone by the type of people they spend their time with and I don't like the guys you're hanging out with." At the time, I thought she just didn't like my friends, which was true to a certain extent—not because she had anything against my friends; she just thought I could do better if I hung around better people. It took me about forty years to realize that what she was saying is one of the most fundamental laws of success. Grandma was right!

Develop a Pleasing Personality.

People like to be around people who make them feel good. Who wants to be around *anything* nasty or irritating, let alone a negative, unpleasant person? Would you rather hang around a garbage dump or a flower garden? *Be nice.* Talk nice, smell nice, act nice, and like magic, people will want to be around you.

Position Yourself.

Put yourself in the position to meet the "right" people. First, determine who you want to connect with, find out where they hang out, and go there. Some of the more obvious places include the golf course, professional and charitable organizations, chambers of commerce, networking events, and so on. You must be involved to be noticed and to meet the people you want to meet.

Make Yourself the Connection.

Instead of spending your time trying to connect, become the connection. Make yourself the person everyone wants to meet. How? Do what you're great at; do it a lot; let everyone know that you're doing it, where you're doing it, and when you're doing it.

Become an Expert.

Make yourself the go-to person by writing, blogging, and speaking about your industry. Provide solutions to the common problems people and businesses are facing, and you will become a sought-after expert in your field.

Serve First.

I got this little nugget from my friend Larry Broughten at one of Craig Duswalt's RockStar Marketing Boot Camps in L.A. Those two little words resonated with me. I was contemplating ways to improve on my accounting craft and these two words helped increase my revenue by over 30 percent in one year. Serving first works, works well, and works 100 percent of the time.

Take $Money$ Out of the Equation.

Go out there and do the stuff you do without any expectation of compensation, monetary or otherwise. There are many ways to accomplish this if you think about it. Don't serve just for the exposure, although exposure is not a bad thing. Serve because you're willing to work and show value before you ask to be paid.

Recently, one of my largest clients was struggling financially. They needed my help, and I knew exactly what needed to be done. They didn't ask me to work for free and I had no intention of working pro bono. I just knew that if I did what needed to be done, I would be compensated accordingly. Not only did my revenue from the client increase; I have become an integral part of their growth and success.

The money is good, but the satisfaction that I was able to help the client grow and succeed is the kind of satisfaction that really drives me.

How has this helped me make more quality connections? The ripple effect of doing the right thing helped open doors to individuals and opportunities that wouldn't have existed had I simply just done what they were paying me for.

Go the extra mile, and the "connections" and unbelievable rewards will always follow. That is an indisputable fact!

CHAPTER 5

Myth #4

A Bad Economy

If you think the economy is the reason for your business troubles, you are 100 percent correct. Actually, your thinking is what makes it a reality. When people believe there is a problem, the problem becomes reality. If you believe the economy is bad, it is a certainty that it will affect your business. Successful people buy when prices are low. The only way people lose in a bad market is when they sell. Successful people understand that markets go up and down, and they don't panic when it's down. In fact, many of them see the low points as buying opportunities. History proves that eventually, no matter how low it goes, the market always come back. It's just a matter of time. The fear of loss often causes the loss. Your dominant thoughts are what drive you. If you let the bad economy dominate your thoughts, you are driven by fear. Fear blocks us and clouds our mind in a way that when an opportunity presents itself, we are not able to recognize it.

The truth is that opportunities exist everywhere, all the time, even when the economy has apparently gone south. The economy operates on a cycle. It goes up and it goes down. Very few people can successfully predict when and to what extent it will fluctuate. The only constant is the fact that it will inevitably fluctuate. Why then, if we know that something is going to happen, do we still act with shock and dismay? It's like feeling bad because the sun is going down.

Solutions to a Bad Economy

Stay Away from the Naysayers.

The law of attraction works both ways. If you believe that like attracts like, then being around negativity will attract more negativity.

Surround Yourself with Positive People.

See above. Positivity breeds positivity.

Develop the Habit of Saving.

The real issue is not whether the economy will experience a downturn; it's our lack of preparation for it that hurts. Start socking away money for when times are lean. Market corrections weed out the marginal businesses, so don't be marginal. Put yourself in the position of being a buyer when opportunities present themselves.

Keep Costs Down.

When business is good and cash flow plentiful, many entrepreneurs get caught up in the delusion that it will always be this way. Foolish entrepreneurs start making long-term commitments; buying fancy cars; going on long, expensive vacations; and trying to expand too rapidly. Don't commit to expensive contracts or increase your overhead.

Ask yourself these questions when making a purchase:

- Do I want this or do I need this?
- Is this costing the company money or saving the company money?
- Is this adding to or subtracting from our bottom line?
- How is this going to affect our overhead?
- Can we do without this right now?

CHAPTER 6

Myth #5

Lack of Business Knowledge

There are scores of brilliant professors of business who never achieved any real business success. One of the most successful stock traders I ever met worked in a steel factory. Ninety percent of all the stocks he bought were sold at a profit. When I asked him how he did it, he said, "I listen to the news." He bought stocks of companies that provided the staples of life such as food and clothing. When their stocks were low, he bought; when they went up, he sold. He wasn't greedy and used simple common sense.

Henry Ford's Famous Lawsuit

There is a story about an episode that occurred during Henry Ford's libel lawsuit against the *Chicago Tribune*. The *Tribune*'s lawyers pounded Mr. Ford with a multitude of repetitious questions about history, aiming to show Mr. Ford's ignorance and lack of knowledge. They believed that this knowledge should be required of anyone with such power and wealth. The tale has it that after many seemingly inconsequential questions, Mr. Ford slapped the table in front of him and asked, "Why would I fill my mind with such useless information when it serves no purpose in running my business? On my desk, I have a row of buttons that enable me to summon the most brilliant minds available whom I need to operate my business. If I need knowledge about any subject, I simply push a button and have it at my disposal."

Truth be told, this never actually happened. It's folklore, but it illustrates a point about intelligence versus knowledge. Mr. Ford was actually unworldly and uneducated. He confused the War of 1812 with the American Revolution and thought that Benedict Arnold was an author.

In some respects, Mr. Ford was perhaps not the sharpest blade in the drawer. Does this diminish his standing as one of the greatest businessmen and industrialists who ever lived? I think not. In fact, in my eyes, it magnifies his persona and genius. In fact, it shows that a lack of knowledge, even business knowledge, never stops anyone from achieving success. The belief that a lack of knowledge could stop them is what actually stops them.

Solutions to a Lack of Business Knowledge
Use Basic Common Sense.

Sometimes we tend to overthink things. The most ingenious solutions are the simplest. Case in point: As a CPA,

I was trained to reconcile bank accounts every month. Bank statements were available to account holders when the banks mailed them at the end of the monthly cycle. Technology changed all that. We can now access accounts online, 24/7.

During 2004, I developed a remote bookkeeping system that leveraged the latest technology. My clients provided on-line access to their bank accounts, and I taught my mom how to reconcile the way I always did it, at the end of the month.

One Saturday, she decided to do the bank recs, even though it was only one week into the month. She called me to let me know that an account belonging to one of my clients was overdrawn, and if he didn't get cash into the account by Monday, he might start bouncing checks. I was confused. Why did she do the reconciliation after only one week had elapsed? Her answer was simple: "Why do I have to wait till the end of the month when the information is available now?"

This was a game changer! It became *real time,* as if we were in the clients' office, taking care of their books. No longer would we be the historians informing the clients after the fact that they had bounced checks. Most of the time, we were giving them information that they already had. The way I marketed the business changed completely, all because Mom used basic common sense. She had no real bookkeeping experience but actually changed my busi-ness absolutely, positively for the better. How did a retired great-grandmother, my mom, provide me (a CPA with over twenty years of experience at the time) with this simple, game-changing idea? She used a very powerful tool: common sense.

Create a Mastermind.

One of the most powerful concepts Andrew Carnegie shared with Napoleon Hill was what he called the *Mastermind,* detailed in the section that follows.

The Mastermind

In 1908, a young Napoleon Hill asked Andrew Carnegie a simple question: "To what do you attribute your success?" Carnegie answered, "Well, if you want to know how I got my money, I will refer you to these men here on my staff; they got it for me. We have here in this business a Mastermind. It is not my mind, and it is not the mind of any other man on my staff, but the sum total of all these minds that I have gathered around me that constitute a Mastermind in the steel business."

What is a Mastermind? Simply put, it is the blending of two or more minds in a spirit of perfect harmony. There is a "mind chemistry" that exists and is made of the same "stuff" as energy. Our brains act as a sort of radio tower, sending and receiving information transmissions. Thought energy is like a radio wave being broadcast. When two or more people harmonize their thoughts, the wave becomes stronger, more powerful. In fact, the energy (thoughts) being transmitted could not have been created by any one individual.

The *Mastermind* is the term Andrew Carnegie coined and Mr. Hill used to describe this phenomenon. The more individuals and the more focused the idea, the more powerful the Mastermind becomes. Successful people have a certain mind-set and attitude. They are positive thinkers who usually have other like-minded individuals close by. Steve Jobs had Steve Wozniak and together they formed Apple Computer. Bill Gates had Paul Allen and together they formed Microsoft. There are endless examples, and I'm sure you have had your own experiences with Masterminds without even realizing it. What you must understand is the fact the Mastermind is a very powerful force that *anyone* can utilize.

Forming a Mastermind Alliance

Once you have your goals set, you should start looking for candidates to create your Mastermind alliance. You must be very careful who you choose, because any kind of negative influence will be counterproductive. Start with one person who is close to you who has your best interest in mind. It does not have to be someone even associated with your business. It could be a business mentor to start out with, but eventually you will want to surround yourself with individuals who can be a permanent part of your Mastermind alliance.

The way you can approach the subject is to simply invite the party to discuss some of your business ideas and get some of their feedback and their ideas on how they see it. Most people will be flattered that you respect them enough to start talking openly about your business. You may be surprised how easy it will be to get started. Remember that this has to be a person you can trust and share confidential business information with. The person should be open-minded and flexible. When you start realizing tangible results from your alliance, you can put a name to what you have been doing.

I created many Mastermind alliances even before I knew there was a name for them. I have several Mastermind alliances within my business at the time of this writing. Some know that they are a part of it, while others have no idea. Sometimes we call them staff meetings! I have created a Mastermind alliance with all my employees, and it is one of the most powerful tools I have ever been provided with. What makes it a Mastermind and not just a "staff meeting" has more to do with how it's run and what my people bring to the table than with what it's called.

Our staff meetings are run with an agenda based on where we left off the last time. It's done over the Internet and is very informal and fun for everyone. As we go through the agenda, I ask for feedback and ideas from everyone. Every member of our team is at the same level of participation. What I mean by that is for every item on the table, any member can voice opinions, concerns, and ideas on the subject. From our name and logo to what products and services we provide and how we market them—all have come from our Mastermind!

Your Mastermind alliance does not have to be people in business or with years of business experience. Sometimes a layperson, or even your mother, can provide amazing insight.

Starting the Mastermind

OK, you have chosen your Mastermind cohorts and now you want to begin. Where do you start? You are going to start right at the beginning with some questions: What exactly are you trying to accomplish? What is your vision? What is your Definite Chief Aim? This is where you have to start sharing these ideas.

If you want to open a bar and grill, don't start spewing all your plans, including the potential location, name, and what's going to be on the menu. This is not a Mastermind. The concept of the Mastermind is to take two or more individuals and develop perfectly harmonized ideas. If they are all your own ideas, there is no chance for harmonization.

This is the way to approach it: "I would really appreciate your input on this idea I've had about opening a bar and grill. What do you think?" *It's as simple as that.*

You want to—need to—hear the other person's response and ideas. You start brainstorming.

They may say something like, "A bar and grill? That's great! I always thought you should have a business. Where are you thinking about opening?"

You say, "I'm not sure, I had three locations in mind. What do you think of these?"

When you approach it this way, ideas will emerge that neither of you would have had alone. Together you have formed one of the most powerful business tools available: the Mastermind.

Surround Yourself with Successful People You Know, Trust, and Respect, and Ask for Their Advice.

Successful people know their weaknesses and plug the holes with other people. Andrew Carnegie called it a Mastermind, and today the term is used all over the world for one reason. It works!

Start Educating Yourself.

If you lack knowledge, start acquiring it. It's not going to come to you through osmosis; you have to take the initiative. Books, audio recordings, seminars, webinars, podcasts, online courses, live courses with teachers and students—the world is at your fingertips today. You can learn just about anything from anywhere at any time. Go to YouTube and type in "learn how to . . ." and see what comes up.

CHAPTER 7

Myth #6

Too Much Competition

If you worry about what the competition is doing instead of about what you're supposed to be doing for the success of your own business, you are more likely to fail. When Home Depot opened, I saw a lot of small businesses fail; I believe it was just out of sheer panic. Once again, it's that four letter word that starts with F_ _ _!

F E A R is the real culprit of business failure. If you *fear* the competition, the competition will defeat you! Home Depot sold thousands of products at really low prices. How could anyone compete with them?

The answer is twofold. First, the businesses that focused on themselves, not the competition, were able to hold their own. Business owners who have a creative mind-set are continuously focusing on improvement, innovation, and longevity. There is no time to worry about anything else.

The second part of the answer is *service*. You see, it was hard to find people in the megastore to actually help all the customers they attracted. Many of the customers who initially went to Home Depot returned to the small, local suppliers who knew and cared about their customers and understood that they had a vested interest in helping them. To Home Depot, customers were a commodity that they measured through ROI. The stores are run by a large corporate operation. It's hard to get close to your customers when the people making decisions are thousands of miles away and those customers know the sales clerks only by their name tags.

Solutions to Too Much Competition

Embrace the Creative Mind-Set.

Cocreate with God, your Mastermind, customers, and your peers. We are here to create, not decimate.

Know and Understand Your Customers/Clients.

Invest your resources in learning as much as you can about the people you want to serve. This knowledge and understanding will be invaluable.

Give Up the Competitive Mind-Set.

Instead of competing for the same business, start focusing on creating new business. Stop focusing on what *they* are doing and start thinking about what *you* are doing. Use your competitive nature to be great instead of just beating the guy next door.

Approach Business with an Open Mind.

If some of those businesses that closed looked at Home Depot as an opportunity rather than an adversary, maybe they could have capitalized on the presence of the big orange box. Partner with your "competitors." That's right— instead of competing for business, work together to strengthen one another's businesses.

What Is Competition?

According to Wikipedia, "Competition in biology, ecology, and sociology is a contest between organisms, animals, individuals, groups, etc., for territory, a niche, or a location of resources, for resources and goods, for prestige, recognition, awards, mates, group or social status, or leadership; it is the opposite of cooperation. It arises whenever at least two parties strive for a goal that cannot be shared or is desired individually but not in sharing and cooperation."

What Is Capitalism?

According to Wikipedia, "Capitalism is an economic system that is based on private ownership of the means of production and the creation of goods or services for profit."

- No competition = monopoly.
- Monopoly is bad.
- Competition spurs innovation.
- Competition is good.

Competition is natural. We are all born with a competitive nature, and I believe that our desire to be the best at what we do is among the things that set us apart from the rest of the animal kingdom.

I submit that in today's world, our concept of competition must be set aside in order to realize the true meaning of capitalism. "The creation of goods and services for profit" can be attained through the joint efforts of our *apparent* competitors. If capitalism is about production that ultimately finds its way to a consumer and the focus is shifted to the consumer, businesses that viewed themselves as competitors may be able to provide better products and services at lower costs.

I am not suggesting that you should forget about the whole idea of competition; just stop looking at the competition as the enemy long enough to find some common ground. Come up with some out-of-the-box solutions that can benefit everyone. Think win-win-win. There are many examples where competitors have "partnered up." The biggest one that comes to mind is when Microsoft invested in Apple Computer when Apple was on the verge of bankruptcy. Here are two of the most famous competitors of all time, Bill Gates and Steve Jobs, joining forces for whose benefit? Everyone's—that's whose. Win-win-win!

Become Better Than Who You Are Today.

Instead of trying to be better, bigger, and stronger than everyone else, strive to improve yourself.

Famous Quotes and Anecdotes

About Success

William Jennings Bryan: "Destiny is not a matter of chance; it is a matter of choice. It is not a thing to be waited for; it is a thing to be achieved."

Helen Keller: "I cannot do everything, but I can do something. I must not fail to do the something that I can do."

Mary Kay Ash: "Don't limit yourself. Many people limit themselves to what they think they can do. You can go as far as your mind lets you. What you believe, you can achieve."

Abraham Lincoln: "Always bear in mind that your own resolution to success is more important than any other one thing."

Mahatma Gandhi: "The future depends on what we do in the present."

Failures?

Henry Ford: While Ford is today known for his innovative assembly line and American-made cars, he wasn't an instant success. In fact, his early businesses failed and left him broke five times before he founded the successful Ford Motor Company.

R. H. Macy: Most people are familiar with this large department store chain, but Macy didn't always have it easy. Macy started seven businesses that failed before finally hitting it big with his store in New York City.

Walt Disney: Today Disney rakes in billions from merchandise, movies, and theme parks around the world, but Walt Disney himself had a bit of a rough start. He was fired by a newspaper editor because "he lacked imagination and had no good ideas." After that, Disney started a number of businesses that didn't last too long and ended with bankruptcy and failure. He kept plugging along, however, and eventually found a recipe for success.

Harland David Sanders: Better known as Colonel Sanders of Kentucky Fried Chicken fame, Sanders had a hard time selling his chicken at first. In fact, his famous secret chicken recipe was rejected 1,009 times before a restaurant accepted it.

Bill Gates: Gates didn't seem like a shoe-in for success after dropping out of Harvard and starting a failed first business with Microsoft cofounder Paul Allen called Traf-O-Data. While this early idea didn't work, Gates's later work did, creating the global empire that is Microsoft.

Soichiro Honda: The billion-dollar business that is Honda began with a series of failures and fortunate turns of luck. Honda was turned down by Toyota Motor Corporation after interviewing for a job as an engineer; he was jobless for quite some time. He started making scooters of his own at home and, spurred on by his neighbors, finally started his own business.

Albert Einstein: Most of us take Einstein's name as synonymous with genius, but he didn't always show such promise. Einstein did not speak until he was four and did not read until he was seven, causing his teachers and parents to think he was slow and antisocial. Eventually, he was expelled from school and was refused admittance to the Zurich Polytechnic School. It might have taken him a bit longer, but most people would agree that he caught on pretty well in the end, given that he won the Nobel Prize and changed the face of modern physics.

Isaac Newton: Newton was undoubtedly a genius when it came to math, but he had some failings early on. He never did particularly well in school, and when put in charge of running the family farm, he failed miserably—so poorly in fact that an uncle sent him off to Cambridge, where he finally blossomed into the scholar we know about today.

Thomas Edison: In his early years, teachers told Edison he was "too stupid to learn anything." Work was no better, as he was fired from his first two jobs for not being productive enough. Even as an inventor, Edison made a thousand unsuccessful attempts at inventing the light bulb. Of course, all those unsuccessful attempts finally resulted in the design that worked.

Orville and Wilbur Wright: These brothers battled depression and family illness before starting the bicycle shop that would lead them to experimenting with flight. After numerous attempts at creating flying machines, several years of hard work and tons of failed prototypes, the brothers finally created a plane that could get airborne and stay there.

Oprah Winfrey: Most people know Oprah as one of the most iconic faces on television as well as one of the richest and most successful women in the world. Oprah faced a hard road to get to that position, however, enduring a rough and often abusive childhood as well as numerous career setbacks, including being fired from her job as a television reporter because she was "unfit for television."

Fred Astaire: In his first screen test, the testing director of MGM noted the following about Astaire: "Can't act. Can't sing. Slightly bald. Can dance a little." Astaire went on to become an incredibly successful actor, singer, and dancer and kept that note in his Beverly Hills home to remind him of where he came from.

Sidney Poitier: After his first audition, Poitier was told by the casting director, "Why don't you stop wasting people's time and go out and become a dishwasher or something?" Poitier vowed to show him that he could make it, going on to win an Oscar and becoming one of the most well-regarded actors in the business.

Theodor Seuss Geisel: Today nearly every child has read *The Cat in the Hat* and *Green Eggs and Ham,* yet twenty-seven publishers rejected Dr. Seuss's first book, *To Think That I Saw It on Mulberry Street.*

Charles Schultz: Schultz's *Peanuts* comic strip has had enduring fame, yet this cartoonist had every cartoon he submitted rejected by his high school yearbook staff. Even after high school, Schultz didn't have it easy, applying and being rejected for a position working with Walt Disney.

Stephen King: The first book by this author, the iconic thriller *Carrie,* received thirty rejections, finally causing King to give up and throw it in the trash. His wife fished it out and encouraged him to resubmit it, and the rest is history. King now has the distinction of being one of the best-selling authors of all time.

J. K. Rowling: Rowling may be rolling in a lot of *Harry Potter* dough today, but before she published the series of novels, she was nearly penniless, severely depressed, divorced, and trying to raise a child on her own while attending school and writing a novel. Rowling went from depending on welfare to survive to being one of the richest women in the world in a span of only five years through her hard work and determination.

Elvis Presley: As one of the best-selling artists of all time, Elvis remains a household name, even decades after his death. But back in 1954, Elvis was still a nobody, and

Jimmy Denny, manager of the Grand Ole Opry, fired Elvis Presley after just one performance, telling him, "You ain't goin' nowhere, son. You ought to go back to drivin' a truck."

Michael Jordan: Most people wouldn't believe that a man often lauded as the best basketball player of all time was actually cut from his high school basketball team. Luckily, Jordan didn't let this setback stop him from playing the game, and he has stated, "I have missed more than nine thousand shots in my career. I have lost almost three hundred games. On twenty-six occasions, I have been entrusted to take the game winning shot, and I missed. I have failed over and over and over again in my life. And that is why I succeed."

Babe Ruth: You probably know Babe Ruth because of his home run record (714 during his career), but along with all those home runs came a pretty hefty number of strikeouts as well (1,330 in all). In fact, for decades, he held the record for strikeouts. When asked about this, he simply said, "Every strike brings me closer to the next home run."

Special Offer

According to Andrew Carnegie, the starting point for success is a Definite Chief Aim, as he explained to Napoleon Hill when describing his philosophy of success. Hill studied and documented this philosophy in his first book, *The Law of Success*. In it, he provided a precise formula for success that, over the past century, has been proven to work. It made Hill and many others very, very rich. The precise formula is called a Definite Chief Aim.

Develop Your Own Definite Chief Aim.

I will provide a free consultation to help you develop your own Definite Chief Aim. For more information on this special offer, go to www.MyDefiniteChiefAim.com.

There is a Definite Chief Aim worksheet at the end of this book you can use as a starting point. I highly recommend that you use it. Don't think about your answers; write the first thing that comes to mind. Experience has shown me that works best.

Crafting a Definite Chief Aim is not an easy task. It requires a lot of self-examination. The important thing to remember is that this is just a first draft. You can edit it any time you like.

What Is a Definite Chief Aim?

There are three distinct parts to it:

1. Where?
2. How?
3. What?

Where are you going, *how* are you going to get there, and *what* will the result(s) be?

Bruce Lee's Definite Chief Aim

> "I, Bruce Lee, will be the highest-paid Oriental superstar in the United States. In return, I will give the most exciting performances and render the best quality in the capacity of an actor. Starting in 1970, I will achieve world fame, and from then onward till the end of 1980, I will have in my possession $10 million. I will live the way I please and achieve inner harmony and happiness."
>
> **—Bruce Lee, January 1969**

This is a very powerful example of a Definite Chief Aim. Bruce Lee achieved all his goals and so can you. But first, you must find your own Definite Chief Aim.

Let's dissect Mr. Lee's statement into the three areas I have identified.

Where

"I, Bruce Lee, will be the highest-paid Oriental superstar in the United States."

Bruce Lee defined, in one very clear, concise sentence, where he was going. Does it seem as if there was any doubt about what his destination was?

How

"In return, I will give the most exciting performances and render the best quality in the capacity of an actor."

Mr. Lee determined that in order to reach the goal he wanted to reach, all he would have to do was give the most exciting performance and render the best quality in the capacity of an actor.

Note here that Mr. Lee decided that he was going to be the highest-paid Oriental superstar. He did not mention being an actor. If his goal was to simply be an actor, he might never have been a superstar. Being an actor was *how* he was going to be a superstar.

What

"Starting in 1970, I will achieve world fame, and from then onward till the end of 1980, I will have in my possession $10 million. I will live the way I please and achieve inner harmony and happiness."

A Definite Chief Aim for a Stop Sign

> *"I, Stop Sign, will be a universally recognized symbol of safety. I will stand high on street corners all over the world and be translated into every known language. As a result of my presence, countless lives will be saved, and I will produce hundreds of millions of dollars in revenue for local municipalities. I will instill a sense of peace, harmony, and order everywhere I am displayed."*

Let's review the Where, How, and What of it.

Where—A universally recognized symbol of safety

How—Stand high and be translated into every known language

What—Save countless lives; raise a lot of $$ for municipalities; and instill a sense of peace, harmony, and order

Now, if a stop sign can do it, I'm sure you can do it!

My Definite Chief Aim

I, _____, will (be, become, become known as, create . . .) _____.

In return, I will (give, provide, speak, help, work with . . .) _____.

As a result of my (service, presence, performance, efforts, accomplishments . . .), I will (have, achieve, create, help, provide . . .) _____.

A Definite Chief Aim Worksheet

The purpose of these questions and the following self-analysis is to get your thoughts and feelings on paper as a first step in organizing them into a Definite Chief Aim.

List the three most important things in your life:

1. _____

2. _____

3. _____

List your three favorite activities:

1. _____

2. _____

3. _____

List your top five business goals:

1. _____

2. _____

3. _____

4. _____

5. _____

List your top five personal goals:

1. _____

2. _____

3. _____

4. _____

5. _____

Why did you choose the business you are in?

_____

_____

What do you like about your business?

_____

_____

What do you dislike?

_____

_____

These are self-analysis questions. A big part of developing your Definite Chief Aim is understanding your strengths and weaknesses. A constant self-inventory is required to first define and then maintain your Definite Chief Aim.

- Do you complain often of "feeling bad," and if so, what is the cause?

- Do you find fault with other people at the slightest provocation?

- Do you frequently make mistakes at work, and if so, why?

- Are you sarcastic and offensive in your conversation?

- Do you deliberately avoid association with anyone, and if so, why?

- Do you suffer frequently with indigestion? If so, what is the cause?

- Does life seem futile and the future hopeless to you? If so, why?

- Do you like your occupation? If not, why?

- Do you often feel self-pity? If so, why?

- Are you envious of those who surpass you?

- To which do you devote most thought: success or failure?

- Are you gaining or losing self-confidence as you grow older?

- Do you learn something of value from your mistakes?

- Are you allowing some relative or friend to worry you? If so, why?

- Are you sometimes "in the clouds" and at other times in the depths of despondency?

- Who has the most inspiring influence upon you? Why?

- Do you tolerate negative or discouraging influences that you can avoid?

- Are you careless of your personal appearance? If so, when and why?

- Have you learned how to "drown your troubles" by being too busy to be annoyed by them?

- Would you consider yourself a "spineless weakling" if you permitted others to do your thinking for you?

- How many preventable disturbances annoy you? Why do you tolerate them?

- Does anyone "nag" you, and if so, for what reason?

- Do you have a definite major purpose? If so, what is it?

- What are your plans to achieve your major purpose?

- Do you suffer from any of the six basic fears? If so, which ones?
  - ✓ The fear of criticism
  - ✓ The fear of death
  - ✓ The fear of poverty
  - ✓ The fear of old age
  - ✓ The fear of illness
  - ✓ The fear of the loss of someone's love

- Do you have a method by which you can shield yourself from the negative influence of others?

- Do you use autosuggestion to make your mind positive?

- Which do you value most: your material possessions or the privilege of controlling your own thoughts?

- Are you easily influenced by others against your own judgment?

- Have you added anything of value to your stock of knowledge or state of mind today?

- Do you face squarely the circumstances that make you unhappy, or do you sidestep the responsibility?

- Do you analyze all mistakes and failures and try to profit by them, or do you take the attitude that this is not your duty?

- Can you name three of your most damaging weaknesses? What are you doing to correct them?

- Do you encourage other people to bring their worries to you for sympathy?

- Do you choose, from your daily experiences, lessons or influences that aid in your personal advancement?

- Does your presence have a negative influence on other people as a rule?

- What habits of other people annoy you the most?

- Do you form your own opinions or permit yourself to be influenced by other people?

- Have you learned how to create a state of mind with which you can shield yourself against all discouraging influences?

- Does your occupation inspire you with faith and hope?

- Are you conscious of possessing spiritual forces of sufficient power to enable you to keep your mind free from all forms of fear?

- Do you feel it your duty to share other people's worries? If so, why?

- If you believe that like attracts like, what have you learned about yourself by studying the friends whom you attract?

- What connection, if any, do you see between the people with whom you associate most closely and any unhappiness you may experience?

- Could it be possible that some person whom you consider to be a friend is, in reality, your worst enemy, because of the negative influence on your mind?

- By what rules do you judge who is damaging to you?

- Are your intimate associates mentally superior or inferior to you?

- How much time out of every twenty-four hours do you devote to
  - ✓ your occupation?
  - ✓ sleep?
  - ✓ play and relaxation?
  - ✓ acquiring useful knowledge?
  - ✓ plain waste?

- Who among your acquaintances
  - ✓ encourages you most?
  - ✓ cautions you most?
  - ✓ discourages you most?
  - ✓ helps you most in other ways?

- What is your greatest worry?

- Why do you tolerate it?

- When others offer you free, unsolicited advice, do you accept it without question or analyze their motive?

- What, above all else, do you desire?

- Do you intend to acquire it?

- Are you willing to subordinate all other desires to this one?

- How much time daily do you devote to acquiring it?

- Do you change your mind often? If so, why?

- Do you usually finish what you begin?

- Are you easily impressed by other people's businesses or professional titles, college degrees or wealth?

- Are you easily influenced by what other people think or say of you?

- Do you cater to people because of their social or financial status?

- Who, in your opinion, is the greatest living person?

- In what respect is this person superior to you?

- How much time have you devoted to studying and answering these questions?

Special Added Bonus to Motivate You to Success

Be Tenacious

Larry Broughton

"Suck it up and drive on" was the message I repeated to myself that cold evening in the rural hills of North Carolina— I could not let myself give up. I'd spent the day scrounging for edible plants, bugs, and small animals, but to this point could only come up with a couple of plump worms and a lone grasshopper for nourishment. Anything I could have eaten had either fled or been destroyed by the fire.

In order to complete the survival phase of my journey to become one the military's elite Green Berets, the cadre of the US Army's Special Forces Qualification Course had dropped me off in an area that was to be my home for the next few days. It was my lame luck the forest service had conducted a controlled burn of the area just weeks before, clearing the tall grass and underbrush small animals usually used for shelter. I was sent there to live off the land. My directive and course requirements were to build some sort of shelter and fire and a laundry list of improvised tools and traps that made my inner–Eagle Scout want to run home, crying to mamma. The fire that charred and stripped the area of fuel and food made the tasks even more arduous.

The original class of a couple hundred wannabe Green Berets had already been thinned out during the weeks leading up to the survival phase. Most of the guys who left the program were VWs (voluntary withdraws), or as we simply called them, "quitters." They simply lacked the mental and physical toughness to meet the challenges that were thrown at us. For weeks, we'd been running on one small meal a day while stretching our brains with instructional classes, assessing our physical capabilities with long runs and forced marches through the North Carolina sun and sands, and testing our intestinal fortitude by pushing the limits of our warrior spirit.

The added stress of carrying weapons and full rucksacks on the marches made many candidates pass out due to heat exhaustion or dehydration. We endured training sessions and log-drills in the muddy hand-to-hand combatives pit at 2 a.m., excruciating obstacle courses that made some men cry from pain or fear, and leadership and team-building exercises that were meant to test our capabilities during high-stress situations in combat conditions. No matter what was going on around me, though, no matter how many people were throwing up, passing out, or quitting, I kept repeating to myself, "Just take one step at a time, kid. Just put one dusty boot in front of the other."

It was unseasonably cold that night. I huddled to the warmth and glow of my small fire (built dangerously close to my thatched lean-to hooch), "enjoying" my two fried worms (that were supposed to taste like bacon—they lied) and my grasshopper. I sipped my hot pine-needle tea while peering down at one of the small "tools" we were issued just moments before we were dropped in the forest. It was a book of matches . . . but it wasn't just any book of matches. They were from the popular Winn Dixie grocery store chain found throughout the South. On the front cover was a picture of the most beautiful steak I had ever seen; on the back cover was a smiling pig that looked right at me. I was certain the Cadre distributed these particular matches less as a tool to start a fire (after all, we knew how to do that without matches) and more as a mind game to toy with us during this ~~starvation~~ survival phase of the course.

As I sat there staring into my small fire, a soft rain started to fall. Off in the distance I heard a muffled "pop," and I jumped to my feet. A split second later, I saw the light of an aerial flare from one of my fellow candidates. As the brilliant colors lit up the sky, I thought to myself, "quitter." We were each issued a flare that we were meant to deploy in the event we were injured and needed assistance, or if we were ready to VW. I was certain this was a VW, and it meant one fewer guy I had to compete against.

Light-headed and dizzy, due to the quick movement and the lack of food, I leaned against a tree and watched the light from the flare dissipate and listened to the sound of the rain, until a couple of minutes later when I heard another "pop." As the pace of the rain increased, so did the number of flares going off around me. I sat shivering in my hooch, watching the rainfall, dreaming of hot chocolate and warm dry sheets, and enjoying the light show, as if it were the Fourth of July!

+ + + + +

Do you ever wonder how many people quit on something, just short of their goal, not knowing success is right around the corner? I've seen countless early quitters in my life who've thrown in the towel the *first time* they failed at something or when the going got tough. I tend not to have much sympathy for those early quitters. However, my heart breaks most for those who've dug deep inside through difficult times, persevered over and over again, and given up just short of the prize.

My wrestling coach used to bark, "Winners never quit, and quitters never win!" The simple reason some winners never quit is because they'd hate to wake up and realize just one more push could have driven them past their goal. Additionally, they've recognized that failure is a natural part of succeeding; and if they're not failing, then they're not moving fasting enough or getting close enough to their fullest potential.

We must accept that adverse market conditions, competitors, and our own missteps will always seem to get in the way of immediately attaining our goals. Here's the truth: the single most important ingredient, tool, or technique that will ensure enduring success has been a critical piece of the victory equation in arts, industry, politics, and sports for centuries. In a word, it's *tenacity.*

Nothing will serve us better on our journey toward success and significance than the combination of learning from our failures and maintaining a tenacious spirit—simply digging deep, moving forward, outlasting our competition, and hanging on while others let go. Talent, education, and genius, without action and perseverance, will never be a match for the tenacious, never-surrender attitude.

Success requires grit, effort, and hard work. Most folks don't want to commit to that, and so they simply don't succeed (if, that is, they even have the guts to try). Don't focus on them; focus on those who have shown success over and over again. Examine them; exam their technique; examine their team; but most of all, examine their attitude and philosophy on success and failure. After all, success leaves clues.

If you find yourself longing for the "good life," or you feel resentment or jealousy toward those who are living their dreams, it's time to take a look in the mirror. Have you honestly been tenacious in the pursuit of your dreams? How long have you been reaching for that prize? How hard have you really worked for it? You must understand this: most high achievers have sacrificed big time, they manage their shortcomings, they are dogged in their approach, and they want success as much as a drowning man wants air to breathe.

More than any other ingredient, the key to overcoming failure and realizing enduring success is *tenacity*.

So how do we become tenacious? By building our "tenacity muscle." When a weight lifter wants larger, stronger muscles, they increase resistance by lifting heavier weights. When they stop increasing weights, they stop growing stronger. This simple concept is true in other areas of life.

Start by following these five steps: set goals, check your attitude, take action, embrace failure, and never quit.

1. Set Goals.

Surprisingly, goal planning and goal setting are not topics taught at most business schools and universities. I believe in keeping things as simple as possible so we can focus clearly on the prize and are more effective in achieving our goals. There is both empirical and anecdotal evidence demonstrating that writing down our goals enhances goal achievement. So,

    a. Choose the one thing you want to accomplish in the next twelve months. Keep it to one thing, as too many people get bogged down and discouraged by too many goals.

b. Create a two- to five-word mantra to describe your goal (i.e., "Win the Green Beret"). Be sure you are passionate about your goal or you'll lose motivation to pursue it.

c. Write the mantra on index cards and affix them to your bathroom mirror, car dashboard, refrigerator door, and computer screen. Do everything you can to sear your mantra in to your conscious and sub-conscious mind, and repeat it out loud several times each day.

d. Since your primary goal will take specific steps to accomplish, identify smaller subgoals you can complete today, this week, and this month.

Be sure to keep your primary goal to just one thing, at least for now.

Sidebar Tip

Before we go any further, let's get one thing straight: no goal is worth the time, energy, or effort if it's purely self-serving, out of alignment with your core values, or takes a lot of mental and emotional pushing and shoving. The "pushing and shoving technique of goal achievement" (which loosely translates into "getting what I want") has led me, and many other "good people," into wandering the wilderness and wastelands of life. The best goals are those that allow you to serve others while doing what you love, what you do well, what the world needs, and what they're willing to pay you for. Achieving this perfect balance is called "bliss."

2. Check Your Attitude.

Martial artist, actor, and entrepreneur Chuck Norris once said, "You need the tenacity to stick to it when things get tough. And have faith that you can do it." More than anyone else in our world, we have to believe in our own efforts.

We must be tenacious in both our attitude and our actions, because a good attitude won't guarantee victory, but a bad attitude will absolutely guarantee defeat. I've had the honor of knowing and working with people who have achieved their dreams and live lives of significance and abundance. But I know many more who are nowhere near living their ideal lifestyle.

Too often, resentment builds in those who have not achieved the immediate success they've sought. They believe that success came easy or was handed to those who have achieved greatness before them. That kind of attitude will smother any possibility of accomplishing our dreams.

I've learned that those who are living their ideal lifestyle and who have achieved much success have simply taken time to learn from their failures and shortcomings and worked longer and harder than those who are not successful.

Easy success is a reality for very few people. Most find that they strive, struggle, stumble, and sometimes repeat the cycle, then succeed. Rather than getting resentful, let's use the journey toward success as a growth opportunity. Let's view it as our transformation period before our big reveal! If you've not succeeded yet, you're not ready yet. And let's remember it all becomes part of our story to inspire others toward greatness, too.

No matter where you are on your journey, you'll likely find that the two most significant obstacles to your success include your own negative mental chatter and the chatter of other people. You've likely found well-intentioned family members and friends who question your dream and try to convince you to abandon it. Why? Well, they'll tell you they don't want to see you get hurt. The fact is, misery loves company.

So instead of focusing on the negative, we must remain positive and surround ourselves with people who encourage us and want us to succeed. Personal development guru Jim Rohn is famous for saying, "You are the average of the five people you spend the most time with." Look around you and make your own assessment.

Sidebar Tip

Sure, we can easily identify family and friends who negatively speak into our lives, who seem to want to keep us from achieving our goals for one reason or another; but what about that other, more covert, saboteur? Who is that, you ask? Sadly, *we* can be our own worst (most destructive) enemies with all the negative chatter we have going on inside our heads.

We must replace the negative mental chatter we've come to accept as normal, with positive messages of meaning, success, and self-worth. What if you stopped talking to yourself in a negative manner but started to talk to yourself as if you were someone you love?

> "If someone else talked to us the way we often talk to ourselves, we'd slap them."
>
> —Dean Del Sesto

3. Take Action.

One of my favorite quotes pertaining to taking action is by General George Patton, who once said, "A good plan, violently executed today, is better than a perfect plan next week." There are those who fail to take action because they have no plan, while others may overplan or overthink and get stuck in analysis paralysis.

Battles are won, however, and businesses are launched, treasures are found, relationships are restored, and ideas become innovations when dreamers become doers. Our entire lives we've been led to believe the myth that knowledge is power. If we just study harder, learn more, attend another seminar, or read another personal development book, then everything will improve. Stop believing the lie! The truth is, action is power! If you could download every book, manual, and video on Amazon.com directly into your brain but take no action on what you've learned, all that knowledge becomes useless trivia.

Start small if you must, but act like an ant by moving one grain of sand today, another tomorrow, and another the next day. General Patton encourages us to develop a *good* plan, not a *perfect* plan, and not even a *great* plan. Just develop a *good* plan, take action, and make course corrections as you go. The feeling of movement and momentum will be encouraging to you and make the journey easier and more enjoyable.

Success will always evade those who don't take action.

4. Embrace Failure.

Anyone who has ever experienced real success has also experienced moments of failure and hopelessness. Soichiro Honda, the Japanese engineer, industrialist, and founder of Honda Motor Company, believed that "Success is 99 percent failure." Winston Churchill often said, "Success is not final; failure is not fatal. It is the courage to continue that counts."

Understanding that we learn more from our failures than from success, we must fight to avoid the negative chatter about ourselves when our plan goes off course. When our plans go sideways, as they always do, we must assess the situation, take corrective action, learn our lessons, and drive on.

Too often, after a setback, we find ourselves curled in the fetal position, licking our wounds, embracing a victim's mentality. Why is that? Somewhere in human history, we've learned to fear failure. Has that approach ever launched anyone toward his or her goal?

Those who embrace failure are those who accomplish great things and transform the world. Thomas Edison said, "Our greatest weakness lies in giving up. The most certain way to succeed is always to try just one more time."

5. Never Quit.

Publisher William Feather once said, "Success seems to be largely a matter of hanging on after others have let go." I've learned that successful people have simply mastered the art of putting one dusty boot in front of the other, and they just keep driving on!

Thomas Edison failed more than one thousand times before inventing the light bulb. Walt Disney was fired by a newspaper editor who said he lacked imagination and had no good ideas. Michael Jordan was cut from his high school varsity basketball team. Author Jack London received six hundred rejection notices before publishing his first story.

Abraham Lincoln was fired from his job, had two failed businesses, and suffered a nervous breakdown. He ran for office eight times and was defeated before he was elected President in 1860.

Every successful person has faced failure and setbacks on their journey toward success. If we're going to be successful, we're going to face adversity. It's time to accept this as fact and prove that we're tougher than our circumstance. Successful people possess a bullheaded tenacity that gets them through anything.

We must never, never, never quit! Life will be hard, trials will come, and family and friends will "encourage" you to throw in the towel. At that moment, you'll be given a choice: Will you give up, or will you suck it up and drive on? It might not be easy, but it's a simple choice that could impact the rest of your life.

Be Tenacious!

About the Author

Larry Broughton is an author, speaker, award-winning entrepreneur, humanitarian, and family guy. After growing up in a small mill town in rural western New York, he spent eight years with the US Army's elite Special Forces, commonly known as the Green Berets.

Larry has parlayed his unique experience of serving on Special Forces A-Teams to the business world. After serving as Vice President and Partner of one of the country's leading hotel companies, in 2001 he became Founder and CEO of Broughton Hotels (BroughtonHotels.com). Since its inception, his firm has received numerous awards for performance and innovation and is considered a leader in the boutique hotel industry. He has also been awarded Ernst and Young's prestigious Entrepreneur of the Year Award®, NaVOBA's Vetrepreneur® of the Year, Passkeys Foundation's National Business Leader of Integrity Award, Coastline's Visionary of the Year Award, while *Entrepreneur Magazine* named his firm to their Hot 500 List.

Larry has been quoted or featured in news articles across the county, including the *New York Times, Wall Street Journal, USA Today,* and *Entrepreneur Magazine.* He has been a featured guest on national radio shows and on every major television and cable network. He is also a highly sought-after speaker on inspiring topics that impact entrepreneurs, leaders, and high achievers.

For more information on Larry Broughton, please visit www.LarryBroughton.me or www.yoogozi.com.

Resources

www.BedrockBookkeepersOnlineAcademy.com
www.CraigDuswalt.com
www.LarryBroughton.me
www.RockStarPublishingHouse.com
www.yoogozi.com

Suggested Readings

The Science of Getting Rich, by Wallace Wattles
The Law of Success, by Napoleon Hill
The E-myth Revisited, by Michael E. Gerber

www.ingramcontent.com/pod-product-compliance
Lightning Source LLC
Chambersburg PA
CBHW071458210326
41597CB00018B/2604